LEADERSHIP
TRANSITIONS

LEADERSHIP
TRANSITIONS

STEPPING UP TO A CHALLENGING
NEW POSITION

Ronnell D. Crittenden

CONTENTS

About Ronnell D. Crittenden vii

Chapter 1 Welcome to Conglomerated Industries 1

Chapter 2 Cynthia Sees the Challenges............................. 11

Chapter 3 A Very Special Car Takes Cynthia to
Meet a Legend 21

Chapter 4 Lesson One: The Importance of Self-Esteem 31

Chapter 5 Lesson Two: Learning from Mistakes
and Failures 43

Chapter 6 Lesson Three: Understand Your Story............... 55

Chapter 7 Lesson Four: Building Coalitions 65

Chapter 8 Lesson Five: Great Customer Service................. 75

Chapter 9 Lesson Six: Concentration and Focus 85

Chapter 10   A New Day.. 97

Thank You—And Please Spread the Good Word!................. 99

ABOUT RONNELL D. CRITTENDEN

A man who believes there are no limits to human abilities, Ronnell D. Crittenden encourages people from all walks of life to push themselves out of their comfort zones and execute on their ideas while challenging conventional thinking. Ronnell's High Performance philosophy and charismatic personality inspire others to become world class in their chosen fields.

Born in Chicago, Illinois in 1971 and based in Florida since 2001, Ronnell has been an entrepreneur since childhood. At the age of twelve, Ronnell decided to accompany his father on his delivery routes to deliver telephone books door to door in his south side neighborhood. Ronnell graduated from Tilden High School in Chicago and attended Loyola University Chicago, where he studied sociology and anthropology.

Ronnell began his career working for Lakefront SRO, a developer of affordable housing. In 2006, Ronnell began working for Educational Services of America, the nation's leading provider of Pre-K-12 alternative and special education. It was at ESA where Ronnell was exposed to mergers and acquisitions and became fascinated about the concept of how one company can acquire other companies. Ronnell set out on a mission to understand how mergers and acquisitions work. He decided to become a student of mergers and acquisitions by receiving training and mentoring from experts in the areas of Private Equity, Negotiations, Corporate Presentation Development, and High Performance Psychology.

In 2009, Ronnell formed The InspireU Group Inc. a program that provides residential services, transition services, and behavioral services for teen males in foster care. After attending an executive education course on mergers and acquisitions at the University of Minnesota in 2013, Ronnell discovered the transition services he provides at The InspireU Group Inc. are parallel to the experiences of entrepreneurs when they transition from the established stage to the growth stage. After recognizing this discovery, Ronnell decided to develop and redefine his strategy naming it the CEO Strategy.

In 2014, Ronnell founded BridgeView Equity Partners LLC. Ronnell's commitment to lifelong learning led him to the University of Oxford-Said Business School, where he completed the Oxford Private Equity Program and Oxford Chicago Valuation Program from 2016-2017. Ronnell continued his studies at Harvard University-Harvard Law School and completed the Program on Negotiation in 2017.

CHAPTER 1

WELCOME TO CONGLOMERATED INDUSTRIES

With a smile, the man extended his hand. "It's good to see you again, Cynthia, especially on your first day as our new CEO. I hope your flight was pleasant and you've had a chance to settle into your hotel."

"It's good to see you, too, George," she replied as she shook his hand. "When I left Los Angeles it was ninety-five degrees. Here in Chicago the temperature is much more comfortable."

"Wait until January, when the arctic wind comes howling off Lake Michigan!" he laughed.

For a moment they stood in the gleaming lobby of the majestic Conglomerated Building. "I want to thank you and the board's search committee for being so kind to me," said Cynthia. "I can hardly believe that after six months of interviews it's over—or rather I should say, it's just beginning."

"Exactly," said George. "We're focused on the future!" With his hand he motioned towards the bank of elevators. "The board meeting begins in ten minutes. You know, of course, that Mr. Paulson is always quite punctual. It would be wise to be in the room a few minutes before nine o'clock."

As they stepped into the elevator, Cynthia smiled. "I've learned the chairman is a no-nonsense man. But that's good—I suppose it's the reason Conglomerated has only gotten bigger since it was founded in 1920."

"I see you know the company history," said George approvingly as the elevator sighed upward towards the fortieth floor.

"An illustrious history it is!" she replied. "The Paulson family has much to be proud of. It's not easy to keep a private family business going these days, especially one as expansive as Conglomerated."

The elevator doors opened and they stepped into the reception area. Cynthia liked the understated elegance of the Conglomerated Building—it showed her that the company valued performance, not ostentation. They walked through a set of double doors into the board room, where men and women stood around the massive conference table and its leather-backed chairs.

George quickly introduced Cynthia to the few board members who hadn't yet met her. At precisely nine o'clock, with the sun now well into the sky over the shimmering lake,

Mr. Paulson entered the room. He found Cynthia, welcomed her and shook her hand, and without further chitchat indicated she should take her place at the table. Then he took his seat.

After a few preliminary agenda items—introductions and approving the previous meeting's minutes—Mr. Paulson officially welcomed Cynthia to Conglomerated Industries.

"I understand," he said by way of breaking the ice, "that while you're a native of California, you're no stranger to the great city of Chicago."

"Yes, that's true," she replied. "My aunt lived here, and every year or so I'd come with my parents for a visit. We'd visit the Sears Tower—now of course called the Willis Tower—and go to the Lincoln Park Zoo. I was fascinated by the elevated trains and the Museum of Science and Industry. Then after graduating from college I attended Northwestern University for my MBA. It was a wonderful experience, and I studied the titans of industry in Chicago—people like investment industry pioneer, John W. Rogers, the founder of Ariel Investments and J. B. Pritzker, managing partner and co-founder of the Pritzker Group, the big private investment firm. Their stories have inspired me to set my sights high, and I could not be more pleased and honored to take the helm of this great company."

"And we're very glad to have you on board," smiled Mr. Paulson. "Now let's get down to business. Julia, let's hear your report."

"Yes, sir," said a woman in a grey business suit. Cynthia had met Julia Wentworth, the chief financial officer. Cynthia had gotten the impression that she was very tough.

"Our projections for the end of this year are not encouraging," Julia began. "The good news is that grain prices are holding steady, and exports of corn and soybeans to China are expected to increase by three percent. However, steel is underperforming and feeling pressure from new mills in Mexico. Livestock is down five percent from the previous fiscal year. Our food ingredients division was hurt by weather issues, and poultry is down due to the contamination scandal at our operation in Thailand."

"How about our financial services arm?" asked George.

"That's next on our list," replied Julia. "Our insurance company has been hit by a record number of claims from weather events, and regulators in the Eurozone are tightening up. Our outside auditors are recommending that we exit the insurance market. Our brokerage division is performing well because of the growing number of retirees who need financial planning."

"And hotels and leisure?" asked another board member.

"We entered the hotel market ten years ago with a controlling investment in fifty business travel hotels in the United States and Europe. We hope to see a profit next year."

"Ten years and still no profit?" asked Mr. Paulson.

"As the board will recall, the hotels—all part of a chain— needed significant capital improvements. We put three hundred million dollars into renovations. But the business travel market has been soft and our occupancy rate has been only seventy percent when our goal has been eighty percent."

To Cynthia, none of this came as a surprise. Towards the end of her six-month interview process with multiple committees and division heads, she had been asked to sign a non-disclosure agreement, which she had taken as a sign that her candidacy was progressing. After she had signed, the gloomy financial outlook for the company's many divisions was revealed to her. She knew she was stepping into the leadership of a very big company that needed to turn its numbers around.

Mr. Paulson then recognized a man whom Cynthia had not yet met.

"For those of you who don't know me," the man began, "I'm Charles Gregorio, consultant for Apex Business Services. A year ago, the leadership of Conglomerated Industries asked us to perform a top-to-bottom management review. No stone was to be left unturned. I would like to present the results of our study." An assistant handed each board member, including Cynthia, a thick binder. "We plan on reviewing each part of the study with the relevant division heads and, of course, the new CEO," said Charles, with a nod towards Cynthia. "But here's the overview. We found that the management structure of Conglomerated Industries is rigid and, frankly, outdated. There are too many silos and centers of power. Internal communications is poor. Each of the divisions is being operated as if it were an independent company—that is to say, we're not leveraging the resources and size of Conglomerated to produce greater efficiency. Furthermore, we believe that Conglomerated has become too diversified. Remember what Jack Welch said when he took over General Electric in 1981: that in every market it entered, GE was going to be either number one or number two. If the company couldn't do that, it was going to exit that market."

Mr. Paulson fixed his laser-like gaze on Cynthia. "What do you say? Do you agree with that approach—that Conglomerated must be number one or number two in the markets we enter, or get out?"

Every eye in the room turned to her. She felt their pressure.

"Yes, sir, in principal I agree completely," said Cynthia, almost without thinking. "Number one or number two, or we're out—but only after we become convinced we can't rise any higher. I would not want to prematurely throw in the towel."

"Of course not," said Mr. Paulson. He turned to Charles. "What's the recommendation of Apex Business Services regarding the hotel and leisure division?"

"We recommend divesting," he replied. "We think Conglomerated can break even. Sell it for what you've put into it."

"Including the family water parks?" asked Aretha Cooke. Cynthia remembered that the family water park business had been a pet project of hers. For some reason, Aretha—a distant Paulson cousin who owned a hefty share of the company—thought water parks were the family entertainment idea of the future. She had single-handedly persuaded the board to invest hundreds of millions of dollars into a nearly bankrupt chain.

Charles glanced at Mr. Paulson, who gave him a little nod, before turning to Aretha. "Yes, we would recommend divesting the Mega Wet World chain. We see no path to profitability."

"That's because you can't see *clearly*," snapped Aretha. "It's a huge market! Did you know that last year over two million people visited Disney's Typhoon Lagoon in Orlando? Over *two million!* Tickets are sixty-five dollars apiece. That gives Disney one hundred and thirty million dollars in ticket sales, not including selling the visitors food and drinks, and the parking fees."

"Here she goes again," muttered a board member under his breath.

"Aretha," said Mr. Paulson with practiced politeness, "please remember that the people in the Disney Company are experts in family entertainment! It's their core business!"

"You're wasting your breath," said another board member.

"Personally, I think we should invest *more* in Mega Wet World," said George. "I see it as being a cornerstone of a new market for us."

Mr. Paulson shot him a stern glance.

"Well, I'm glad *somebody* on this board has some sense!" proclaimed Aretha.

Cynthia knew that if Aretha and George could ally themselves with only two or three other board members, they would have enough ownership clout to give Mr. Paulson a real headache.

Mr. Paulson turned his eyes to Cynthia. "Your thoughts?"

"The board will forgive me if I take some time to study the issue further," she replied diplomatically.

"Giver her a break—it's her first day on the job!" interjected a board member.

"I'd be happy to bring you up to speed," offered Aretha.

"Thank you," replied Cynthia.

"I don't know why we're wasting so much time and money on *water parks*," said an older woman who hadn't spoken yet. Cynthia had met her only once. Ruth Paulson was the great-granddaughter of one of the founders of the company, Elijah Paulson. She wasn't very active in the company—her main interest was the art museum she was building on Chicago's South Side. But she owned a hefty chunk of Conglomerated stock, and even though many of the other board members thought she was an old crank, when she spoke they listened.

"Ruth, my dear," said Mr. Paulson with kindly patience, as if he were speaking to his own mother, "We're discussing it because Mega Wet World was, and continues to be, a significant investment and opportunity for this company."

"Do I have to remind this board," retorted Ruth, "That nearly a century ago, Elijah Paulson was interested in feeding his neighbors and building safe houses for them! Those are things that mattered! Now we're getting involved in swimming pools! Why?"

"Folks," said Mr. Paulson, "Let's calm down. We have a lot on our plates. I'm sure we'd like our new CEO to wave a magic wand and fix all of these problems, but of course we know that's not possible. We need to be patient. We also know that our founder, Elijah Paulson, was a tough, pragmatic businessman, and we need be just as tough as he was. We need to do what's best for Conglomerated Industries and our many customers. Thank you—this meeting is adjourned."

CHAPTER 2

Cynthia Sees the Challenges

C ynthia spent the rest of the day being guided from one office to another in the towering Conglomerated Building. She met people in marketing, research and development, human resources, finance, operations, compliance, the travel office. She met the managers responsible for the various business lines—corn, soybeans, biofuels, steel and ferrous metals, food products such as starches and vegetable oils, livestock, poultry, bakery products (The "Little Miss Paulson" line of snack foods), financial products, and hotels and leisure.

The vice president in charge of Mega Wet World occupied an office on the twenty-fifth floor. His name was Jerome Wheatley. He oversaw an office of thirty or so employees, who together served as the corporate face of the seven Mega Wet World locations.

Jerome, who seemed nice but nervous (perhaps he had heard rumors of his imminent demise—but Cynthia, being with her board handlers, couldn't ask him directly), told Cynthia his background was in logistics.

"So you were promoted to vice president of leisure services without any prior experience in the leisure industry?" she asked.

"Business is business," he smiled. "The skills are transferable."

Cynthia said nothing. Jerome introduced her around the office. "This is Marjorie, the human resources manager," he said as a woman stood up. "She oversees a staff of five here in Chicago."

"We approve every hire at all the parks," said Marjorie, with pride.

"Even the people who work at the refreshment stands or who launder the towels?" asked Cynthia. "You personally approve all of them?"

"Yes," replied Marjorie, this time with a bit less bravado because she sensed vague disapproval from the new CEO.

Cynthia made no reply, but nodded with a polite smile.

"And here's our marketing director, Tim Short," said Jerome.

Tim shook Cynthia's hand. "I've seen your ads on television," said Cynthia. "Nice work. What's your social media strategy? Facebook, Instagram, Twitter?"

"We're not really there yet," replied Tim. "You see, Conglomerated has traditionally been a B2B company. We've never sold directly to consumers. Aside from Little Miss Paulson snack foods, which is operated by a licensee, there are no branded Conglomerated products on store shelves. So it's taken the company leadership a while to understand how to do retail marketing."

"So they approve television ads, which they understand, but not social media," replied Cynthia.

Tim, sensing the cool looks from George and the other board members who were introducing the new CEO around the building, replied, "Well, of course these things take time, and I'm sure we'll soon have a robust social media campaign."

"Who approves your marketing budget and plan?" pressed Cynthia.

Jerome stepped into the discussion. "The budget is approved by the Conglomerated vice president of budget and finance, Roberta Oppenheim. The marketing plan is approved by the Conglomerated vice president of marketing, Kenarol North. They report to the chief operating officer of the consumer products and services division. They're all on the fortieth floor."

"So how much leeway do *you* have?" Cynthia asked Jerome.

"Oh, a lot," replied Jerome with what to Cynthia looked like forced cheerfulness. "But you can't blame the head office for wanting to keep a close eye on what's going on within this very large company!"

"Of course," replied Cynthia. "Tim, let me ask you one more question. Are there any issues or questions that you've passed up to the fortieth floor, for which you've received no answer?"

Tim glanced nervously at his boss Jerome and the board members. "Uh, well, I don't think so," he said.

"Really?" replied Cynthia. "Not one? Every query gets resolved immediately?"

"It takes time," conceded Tim.

"Give me an example," pressed Cynthia.

"Well, a few months ago Typhoon Lagoon in Orlando introduced 'Disney H2O Glow Nights.' They keep the park open at night, with innovative lighting and a dance party. They target adults with a special area dubbed The Wharf, featuring entertainment, special food items, and a bar with beer and wine. It's quickly become very popular!"

"How do you *know* it's become very popular?" asked Cynthia.

"Because I went there myself to check it out," replied Tim. "I make it my business to visit competing water parks. I like going to water parks with my family. Always have."

"So you went to Typhoon Lagoon yourself?" asked Cynthia.

"I had some vacation time."

"Okay," said Cynthia. "Then what happened?"

"I created a plan to keep Mega Wet World parks open on selected nights, with attractions similar to those at Typhoon Lagoon. The idea is to serve more adults. I've found that our revenue drops significantly after dark, because parents don't bring their kids at night. The answer is to pivot after sunset and go after the adult market. Jerome approved the plan, and then we sent it up to the 'Turtle Twins' for review."

"The *who*?" demanded Cynthia.

"Tim's just kidding," laughed Jerome nervously.

"Come on, tell me—who are the 'Turtle Twins'?" insisted Cynthia.

Tim took a deep breath. "It's really just a silly nickname for Roberta and Kenarol. It's just a joke. We call them that because they're incredibly slow to respond. Like two turtles."

"They said you cannot market to adults at night?" asked Cynthia.

"They never explicitly turned us down," replied Jerome. "They told us it was being *studied*. Week after week, they said it was being *studied*. Then they came back and said that it would be too difficult because of liquor license issues."

"I told them I had researched that question," interjected Tim. "Of our seven Mega Wet World locations, I could get licensing for five of them within a month. The other two would take a few months, but we could do it."

"And?" asked Cynthia.

Tim shrugged. "That was over a month ago. I've heard nothing. We've moved on. What can you do? Obviously they don't want to try it. They just won't go on the record as saying so."

George glanced at his watch. "Oh, we're running behind schedule. We need to be moving along—our next stop is with the vice president of Little Miss Paulson snack foods."

Late in the afternoon, Cynthia had a few minutes break from the whirlwind tour. She went to her new office, and for the first time she sat down at the big mahogany desk. According to company lore, the desk had been used by Elijah Paulson himself when the company bought grains from Midwest farmers and sold them to food products manufacturers on the East Coast. It was said that if you opened the drawers late at night, you could smell the lingering odor of cornmeal.

She picked up her phone and tapped a number.

"Hello, Alex? Cynthia Langford here. Yes, I'm in Chicago. It's my first day as CEO of Conglomerated Industries. Are you free for dinner tonight? Great! How about seven-thirty. You tell me where—anyplace you'd like. My treat."

At seven-thirty that evening, Cynthia's car pulled up in front of The Berghoff. She smiled. It was just like Alex to be given the choice of any gourmet restaurant in Chicago, and for him to say, "You need to go to The Berghoff. It's one of the oldest restaurants in Chicago. Herman Berghoff first opened its doors in 1898, and the place hasn't changed much since. When Prohibition was repealed in 1933, The Berghoff was issued Chicago's very first liquor license. Then for thirty-six years, The Berghoff maintained a separate bar for men only. The segregation ended in 1969, when members of the National Organization for Women, led by Gloria Steinem, stood at the bar and demanded service. So I think it would be fitting that you stand at the bar too."

After paying the driver, she walked in the front door. Inside was unexpectedly grand, with warm wood paneling and a high, beamed ceiling from which hung softly glowing Art Deco lighting fixtures. Alex was waiting for her, and they sat down at a table for two.

"There certainly is a lot of atmosphere here," said Cynthia.

Alex smiled. "You can go to a four-star eatery anywhere, but if you want to know Chicago, this is where you come first. It's all about the people, and if you want to get to know Chicagoans, you come to places like The Berghoff. But tonight is about you. Congratulations! Being named the CEO of one of the biggest privately held companies in America is no small feat. I always knew you were destined for success!"

"You inspired me," she replied.

It was true. Alex Tomlin had been Cynthia's counselor at Northwestern as she wrote her MBA thesis, which was on corporate leadership, and he had introduced her to the stories of many of the great leaders of business. He had been a father figure to her, offering advice not just on the subject matter of her courses but on how to succeed in business.

"How long has it been since I've seen you?" he asked as they perused the menus. "Ten years? But of course I've been following your progress in the news. The first time I read about you was two years after you got your MBA, and you were promoted to regional vice president of Astro Manufacturing. I was not surprised. I knew you had what it took to succeed! And then you were made executive vice president at Astro, followed by CEO of HomeLife Homecenters, the big building supplies company. You held your own in a corporate culture dominated by men."

"Tell me about it!" she laughed. "The first day I was CEO, I convened a meeting of all the top executives, and they were all men. But I did what you told me—I just acted like myself and I stayed focused on business. A few of the older guys gave me a hard time, but I was patient with them and didn't lose my cool. They eventually came around."

"You increased the value of the company by ten percent in your first year!" said Alex. "Very impressive. And then Conglomerated came calling."

"Yes they did, and now here I am, living in Chicago. Or at least in a hotel, until I find a house or a condo. How about you? Are you still teaching at Northwestern?"

"Only one class—in business leadership," replied Alex. "I'm semi-retired. I have a little business on the side."

"What's that?" asked Cynthia.

"Oh, you might call it a limousine service. It's for very special occasions."

"Do you mean like weddings?"

Alex smiled. "No, we haven't done any weddings. It's more of an extension of my teaching."

"I don't understand," said Cynthia.

"I'll show you later on."

Their meals were brought by the server—beef medallions for Alex and the seared halibut for Cynthia. After they had eaten for a while, Alex looked at Cynthia and said, "While I'm flattered that you would ask an old professor to dinner, I think there's more to this than just catching up. Am I right?"

"Yes," she replied. "I'll be honest with you—this Conglomerated job may be more than I can handle. It's a huge global company with serious problems. When I was being interviewed for the position they gave me all the usual financials. I assumed that my job would be to get the margins up and improve our market positions. But today I learned the board wants radical change. Many of the company's divisions are losing money. We're going to have to divest. But perhaps even more significantly, the management structure is sclerotic. It's a dense bureaucracy with rampant silos and turf wars. I saw some of it today, on what was supposed to be a pleasant introductory tour. The people in the leisure division—they operate the hotels and the water parks—described a relationship with the corporate office that sounds dysfunctional. No one in corporate wants to make a decision! So they just say, 'We're studying it,' or, 'We'll get back to you on that.'"

Alex nodded. "The old ways die hard. But I think you can get the job done!"

CHAPTER 3

A VERY SPECIAL CAR TAKES CYNTHIA TO MEET A LEGEND

As dinner concluded with cappuccinos and ice cream, Cynthia called for the check.

"This has been a wonderful evening and I'm so happy to have seen you," she said. "I cannot tell you how grateful I am for your advice."

"Thank you, but I feel like I haven't given you any advice!" replied Alex. "At least nothing of practical value. And you're paying for dinner! So I think that we're not yet 'even,' as you might say. It is I who am in your debt."

"Don't be silly," replied Cynthia. "But as long as you mention it, I'm a bit stressed over this new job. It's a huge transition—not just for me but for the company. I wish I had more experience with problems on this scale. May I call upon you now and then for guidance?"

"Of course," said Alex.

After Cynthia had signed the check they stood up. "Are you busy tonight?" asked Alex. "If you have a few minutes, I'd like to take you on a little tour of downtown Chicago. Show you some of the sights."

"That sounds wonderful, but I really need to get back to my hotel," she replied. "I want to review some company documents and turn in early. I have a busy day tomorrow."

"At least allow me to give you a lift in my car. I think you'll enjoy it."

"All right," conceded Cynthia. She could not imagine what kind of car Alex, an elderly and semi-retired college professor, would own. It didn't matter—a short ride in an old jalopy would be the least she could do to make him happy.

They walked out of the restaurant. The evening air was cool, with a breeze off the water. The street was quiet.

"Where's your car?" asked Cynthia. "In a parking garage?"

"Oh, no," smiled Alex. "My driver is bringing it around."

"Oh—you have a driver?" Cynthia said, trying to not sound surprised.

"It's really a sort of part-time gig. As I mentioned inside, I have a car service for special occasions."

They stood on the sidewalk for a minute, waiting for the car. Then Cynthia's phone rang. She opened her purse and glanced at the caller ID. She didn't recognize the number so she decided not to answer it. She thought it was rude to talk on the phone when you were with someone.

She looked up and there before them, idling by the curb, was a magnificent Rolls-Royce.

"Our chariot awaits," said Alex.

"That's funny—I didn't hear the car approach," replied Cynthia. "It just appeared there."

Alex shrugged. "Rolls-Royce automobiles are known to be exceptionally quiet."

The driver's door opened and a man got out. Dressed in a black chauffeur's uniform complete with a smart chauffeur's hat, he looked to be even older than Alex. But despite his age he moved with surprising agility, and briskly opened the rear door. Smiling, he stood at attention with his hand on the door handle.

"This is Winston, my driver," said Alex. "Winston, please meet Cynthia Langford. She's the new CEO of Conglomerated Industries."

"Congratulations, Ms. Langford," said Winston with a little bow.

Alex followed Cynthia into the spacious rear seat of the car and the door closed softly behind them.

"This is quite a nice car," said Cynthia as she ran her fingertips across the burled walnut trim. "I've never been in a Rolls-Royce before. It's like being in a private compartment on the Orient Express. There's something very old-fashioned about it."

"This Silver Spirit is nearly thirty years old, so I suppose you could call it an antique," said Alex as Winston smoothly nosed the car into the street, like a first-class passenger train imperceptibly picking up speed as it pulls away from the platform. "But it's a very special vehicle and I wouldn't trade it for any other in the world."

"Where did you get it, if you don't mind my asking? I never thought of you as being the Rolls-Royce type. No offense—I hope you know what I mean."

Alex laughed. "No offense taken! You're quite right, in fact. Normally I have no need for ostentatious luxuries. Around campus I'm quite happy to ride my bicycle. But as I said, this is a very special car. It was given to me by a professor who owned it and took very good care of it. But he retired, and asked me to carry on for him."

"Carry on? What do you mean?"

"You'll see. Why don't you look out the window?"

Cynthia glanced out through the thick tinted glass. After a moment she turned to Alex. "What neighborhood is this? It looks funny, like a movie set. All the cars parked along the street are old-fashioned, like this one. And we just passed a row of pay phones! I didn't know pay phones still existed!"

"I told you this car was very special," replied Alex. "In fact, it's a time machine."

"A *what?*"

"It's a bit more complicated, but that's the simplest way to describe it. This car can go back in time to any date *after* it was built. It *can't* go back to a time *before* it was built. That wouldn't make any sense, would it?"

"No, that wouldn't make any sense at all. What year was this car made?"

"This Rolls-Royce Silver Spirit rolled off the assembly line at Crewe, England, on March 30, 1989. Therefore it has the ability to return to any date since then, but not prior."

"Of course," nodded Cynthia. "How could it go back to a time when it didn't exist?"

"Right—it couldn't."

"Would you care to tell me what the date is right now? I mean, out there?" she said as she nodded towards the window.

"It's Wednesday, May 24, 1989."

"And why are we here?"

"Because I want you to meet someone very special, and this happens to be a convenient time for her."

Cynthia glanced at her watch. "Oh, excuse me—do you mind if I make a quick call? I told my broker I'd confirm something with him."

Alex smiled. "Be my guest."

Cynthia tapped her phone. The lights went on and the app icons jiggled, but the call didn't go through.

Alex reached into the center console compartment and withdrew a bulky phone with an antenna sticking out of the top. "You're forgetting—we're in 1989. Your wireless network doesn't exist yet. This new Motorola is the state of the art in cell phone design. It costs only three thousand dollars and has a battery life of seventy-five minutes! Would you like to try it?"

Cynthia eyed the device. "It looks like it belongs in a museum. No thanks—my call wasn't that important. It can wait until we get back. We *are* going back, aren't we?"

"Yes, I can assure you we're going back! Nineteen eighty-nine is a nice place to visit, but I wouldn't want to live here."

At that moment the big car glided to a stop. Winston got out and opened the rear door. Alex stepped onto the sidewalk. He turned to Cynthia, who was still in her seat. "Well, come along! We don't want to be late!"

As she got out of the car Cynthia glanced up at the ornate old building. Over the big bronze revolving doors, a red awning shielded the sidewalk. On the scalloped edges of the awning were emblazoned in gold letters the words Lowry Regency Hotel.

"I remember this hotel when I was a student at Northwestern. It was the most luxurious in Chicago, and a lot of famous people like Muhammad Ali and the Rolling Stones stayed here. But I thought it closed a decade ago."

"Yes, it was sold just after the Great Recession," said Alex. "The new owners turned it into luxury condos." After pushing through the revolving doors they entered the gleaming lobby with its polished marble floor and antique wall sconces. Without hesitation Alex went to the front desk.

"Alex Tomlin to see Rebecca Lowry," he said to the crisply attired front desk attendant.

"Yes, sir, she's expecting you," came the reply. "You'll find the private elevator around the corner." He handed Alex a keycard. "You'll need this to use it. Ms. Lowry's office is on the thirty-second floor."

As they rode upward Cynthia said, "You're taking me to see Rebecca Lowry? You really knew her? Or should I say, *know* her? She's legendary in the hotel business."

"Yes, and she's waiting for us. I think you'll find her to be very gracious."

Indeed, when Alex and Cynthia entered Rebecca's office, the hotel chain CEO immediately stood up, warmly shook their hands, and offered them seats in a small conversation area with sofas and a low table. "I like getting out from behind my desk," she said before turning to Cynthia. "Alex has told me quite a bit about you. I've been looking forward to meeting you."

"But how...?" asked Cynthia. "I didn't call Alex until late this afternoon. He had no idea I was in town."

"Don't worry about the operational details," laughed Alex with a wave of his hand. "The important thing is that we're here now, and Rebecca wants to help you."

"Yes, I do," said Rebecca. "Cynthia, I cannot overstate the importance of having mentors to guide you as your career develops and you assume greater responsibilities. I was very lucky that my father, Raymond Lowry—" she nodded towards a framed painting of a distinguished looking gentleman— "founded the first Lowry Hotel and built it into a thriving business. That was in Atlanta, where I grew up. I started working there when I was sixteen. I was a telephone operator, back when hotels had big switchboards. When a call came in

I'd say in a sing song voice, 'Good morning, Lowry Hotel, how may I assist you?' The person would say whom they wanted, and I'd ring up the room. One day I put through a call to the room of Lena Horne, who answered the phone herself. That was a big thrill! Then I worked in the restaurant as a hostess, and then behind the front desk. Fortunately, I quickly became accustomed to seeing celebrities, and I learned how to speak to them. By the time I graduated from college I knew the hotel business very well. I can tell you this: It's all about people—the people who are your guests and the people who are your employees. Both are equally important.

"I was lucky because my father was my mentor. He helped me build the Lowry Hotel chain, and we now have twelve luxury hotels in the United States and Europe. That's why I'm so pleased to meet you and offer whatever advice I can."

"I sincerely appreciate your time," replied Cynthia.

"You've just been named CEO of Conglomerated Industries," said Rebecca. "Congratulations. I know it's a big step up for you. It would be a big step up for *anyone.* But Alex tells me that there are some special challenges of which you were not made fully aware when you accepted the position."

"The job is bigger than I thought," nodded Cynthia. "The board of trustees has just received a report from a consultant. The report identifies many deep-rooted structural problems with the company, which over the years has grown not organically but by acquisition. They've bought companies in a wide variety of industries—including, I must admit, in the hotel industry."

Rebecca raised an eyebrow. "I hope they know what they're doing. It's a tough business even if you've been brought up in it, as I have."

"I agree. I can appreciate that even under ideal circumstances leading a company like Conglomerated would be challenging. But there are internal conflicts. Distrust among managers, people clinging to power, divisions within the board." She paused. "By the way, this is all confidential, isn't it?"

"Yes, absolutely," interjected Alex. "Besides, don't forget we're in 1989."

CHAPTER 4

LESSON ONE: THE IMPORTANCE OF SELF-ESTEEM

"Tell me, Cynthia," said Rebecca Lowry as they sat in her office on the thirty-second floor of the Lowry Regency Hotel, "Do you truly believe you belong where you are? Is being CEO of Conglomerated a good fit, both for your skill set and for what you want to accomplish in life?"

"Yes—or at least I *think* so," replied Cynthia. "I believe in what the company does. I mean, perhaps not every little thing. We are extremely diversified. At the board meeting today there was a heated discussion about our ownership of a chain of family water parks called Mega Wet World. I found myself thinking, why are we in this business? Is it because it's the pet project of a board member, or because it makes sense with our company's mission?"

"What is the mission of Conglomerated Industries?" asked Rebecca.

"I have it here." Taking her phone from her purse, she scrolled through a series of files. "The mission of Conglomerated Industries is to help people live better lives. We will strive to be a global leader at processing and distributing agricultural and other commodities. Our vision is intended to unite, challenge, and inspire everything we do. We will reinvest a substantial amount of our cash flow to provide needed products and services for our customers, rewarding career opportunities for our employees, and attractive long-term value for our shareholders. Our performance measures are: engaged employees, satisfied customers, enriched communities, and profitable growth."

"I'll be very honest with you," said Rebecca. "That's a pretty vague mission statement. Except for the mention of agricultural commodities, which was the company focus when it was first founded, it sounds like you're saying 'We'll excel at everything we do.' While you can't disagree with the message, its vagueness makes it difficult to keep a sharp focus on what differentiates you in the marketplace. But for now, let's not concern ourselves with that. Addressing the mission statement can come later, once you're more secure in your position."

"I need to choose my battles," said Cynthia.

"Exactly," replied Rebecca. "Now that we're acquainted, let's get started. While you're clearly well qualified for the job of CEO of Conglomerated, I sense from you a slight feeling of insecurity. A lack of confidence. I hope you don't mind me saying this."

"Not at all," smiled Cynthia. "I have problems being assertive. Not in a bossy way—no one wants a dictator—but I tend to defer to others even when I'm not convinced they're right."

"Take for example the issue of the Mega Wet World parks," said Rebecca. "Leisure destinations succeed or fail on the basis of *customer service*. Either you please great numbers of ordinary paying customers or you don't. You must cater to them and make them feel special. Is there *anything* in the DNA of Conglomerated that suggests the company is a leader in this area?"

"To be honest, no," replied Cynthia. "We have very little experience in providing services to retail customers. We've traditionally been a commodities wholesaler, a middleman between producers and manufacturers. No one does it better than we do!"

"When you made your last statement—'No one does it better than we do'—I got a real feeling of pride from you. You sounded more confident, like you were on solid ground. You had greater self-esteem."

"Yes, I think you're right," replied Cynthia. "Why is self-esteem so important?"

Rising from her seat, Rebecca went to a bookshelf and, after scanning the titles, chose one of the volumes. She opened the slender book and, after thumbing through the pages, handed it to Cynthia. "This book is all about the value of self-esteem and how it can make you a better leader. It's yours to keep, but in the time we have remaining I'll give you an overview."

For the next hour—or at least it seemed like an hour to Cynthia, because her watch had inexplicably stopped—they discussed the wisdom of the book.

Defining Self-Esteem

Because it's a word that conveys numerous images, the first task is to define what we mean by "self-esteem," particularly as it applies to leaders.

Self-esteem is often defined as a collection of attributes. The person:

- Feels comfortable with who he or she is.
- Believes they have inherent value as a human being.
- Has the ability to demonstrate that value.
- Is confident in his or her ability to successfully achieve their own measure of success.

Self-esteem isn't about being self-centered, boastful, or domineering. Rather, it's about representing ourselves with quiet confidence, as an equal among equals, and leading others from a position of internal strength. Healthy self-esteem frees us to build positive relationships, deliver greater energy in all that we do, and collaborate with others without weighing everyone down in ego management.

It's a purely subjective attribute. It has nothing to do with your circumstances or the people around you. As Eleanor Roosevelt said, "No one can make you feel inferior without your consent."

Low Self-Esteem Is Personal Insecurity

Low self-esteem manifests itself as personal insecurity in seemingly contradictory ways. Insecurity appears in very boisterous or aggressive personalities, but also in timid or passive individuals. Some people with low self-esteem cover up or overcompensate by being the loudest in the room, while others retreat and are afraid assert themselves in a crowd. It can be seen in sports and physical appearance—a person with low self-esteem may lack physical fitness or be poorly dressed, or they may be perfectly fit but with an unhealthy obsession with perfect body image and physical appearance.

Often, low self-esteem is not easily discoverable until you really get to know someone, and the workplace is where this happens. A CEO who hires you may seem gracious and confident during the hiring process, but once you're on board and have worked with this person for a few months or during a crisis, you discover that because they're insecure and lack confidence, they either become abusive (to appear strong) or are indecisive (because they fear being wrong—a sure sign of low self-esteem).

Self-Esteem and Leadership

Developing self-esteem and leadership qualities may take conscious effort. Leaders often find themselves in uncharted territory, with subordinates and stakeholders looking to the leader for direction while rivals eagerly look for the leader to stumble and fall. To build up the type of self-esteem needed for leadership, the leader needs to understand and accept some key concepts.

1. No matter what you do, you cannot please some people. This is just a fact of life. For example, Cynthia knows that the board of trustees of Conglomerated is split on the idea of owning the Mega Wet World parks. Some board members think it's a very good investment while others think it's terrible. It's unlikely they will ever agree, so whichever way Cynthia leans, one or more of them are going to be unhappy with her and may even try to undermine her.

All great leaders have endured criticism—sometimes warranted and sometimes only because the complainer wants to "bring the leader down a notch." This will never change! As a leader, you should learn how to lead your life according to your principles and goals. Make decisions and know how to stick to them. The more you do this, the better you'll get at it. The thoughtful exercise of your authority will help you raise your self-confidence level and develop outstanding leadership qualities.

2. Practice what you're good at. This will help you understand your inner strengths and make proper use of them. Every person is born with some gifts, and developing these will help you find your source of strength and expand your confidence. Know your core strengths and apply them to help make conditions better.

3. Get advice on what you're not good at. Know when to ask for help or expert advice when you're in unfamiliar territory. It's a sure sign of low self-esteem when a leader refuses to accept professional advice for fear of appearing weak. In reality, the most confident leaders always seek the very best outside advice before making a clear and confident decision.

As Steve Jobs said, "It doesn't make sense to hire smart people and then tell them what to do; we hire smart people so they can tell *us* what to do." That's real self-esteem!

. Accept and enjoy responsibility. The world is full of people who avoid responsibility. These are generally unhappy, insecure people. Developing your own way of thinking and implying it in your actions can help you develop your leadership qualities. There is no greater satisfaction than taking on a challenging project and seeing it through to completion.

5. Be a self-starter. If you are dependent on other people (such as your boss) to spur you into action, you need to learn to start your own engine. Being too reliant on others only lowers your self-esteem, and creates an unhealthy dependence on the choices of people who may not know as much as you or who may not have your best interest at heart. It is important that you make your decisions and understand what is good for you and what is not. This will help you in realizing what you want from life and how you can work to make it possible.

Four Key Characteristics of Healthy Self-Esteem

Here are four key characteristics of leaders who have a healthy level of self-esteem.

1. Leaders with high self-esteem don't need to have all the ideas

Leaders with high self esteem do the opposite: they *solicit* ideas from the people around them. They *expect* that the people around them will have ideas and are ready to offer them. They are eager to accept input from others because they realize that doing so makes them a more effective leader. They recognize that a leader's job is to make good decisions based on the very best available information.

In contrast, leaders with low self-esteem need to make themselves feel important. They spend time justifying their position. One way to do this is to come up with all the ideas themselves. Otherwise, they feel as if they aren't doing their job.

2. Leaders with high self-esteem will listen to bad news.

Accepting good feedback is easy—the weakest and most vain leader will revel in praise and happy news. Negative feedback is much more challenging! Even though a leader with high self-esteem is likely to be impacted by negative feedback, he or she won't let it affect their judgment.

Leaders with high self-esteem can see the long-term goal and will seek ways to correct mistakes. These leaders are self assured, and know that negative feedback doesn't mean they don't deserve to hold their position. They also know that feedback is simply a piece of input which doesn't impact their character.

When bad news is delivered, confident leaders don't "kill the messenger," but listen and take the appropriate action in the proper forum. A strong or overly emotional reaction to a messenger delivering bad news stifles open communication—and when a problem arises, open communication is extremely important.

A willingness to hear the bad news keeps leaders from being isolated from critical feedback. When they get information from a variety of sources, across functions and levels, they are more fully informed and can make better decisions.

At Conglomerated Industries, when Cynthia asked Tim if there had been any issues or questions he had submitted to the executives on the fortieth floor for which he had received no answer, she really wanted to know the truth, whether it was favorable or unfavorable. You cannot improve what you don't openly discuss.

3. Leaders with high self-esteem delegate.

They delegate for many reasons, and one of them is that when you give a subordinate a task, it shows that you have trust and confidence in them. Being trusted to complete an interesting and challenging job raises self-esteem, and if your subordinates have strong self-esteem, they'll be motivated to accomplish their goals and go the extra mile for the organization. Delegating tasks to subordinates keeps them engaged, increases company loyalty, and reduces attrition.

4. Leaders with high self-esteem support their teams.

Leaders with high self-esteem believe in themselves and their teams, and make this known to every employee. High self-esteem allows you to make the tough decisions that people expect from a strong leader, and demonstrations of decisiveness are reassuring to your employees. Confidence allows you to lead meetings with authority, to encourage open communication, and foster faith in the company and its mission.

As the discussion was wrapping up, Alex glanced at his watch. "Rebecca, we sincerely thank you for your time and your valuable insights, but we really must be going. I don't want our carriage to turn into a pumpkin!" In response to Cynthia's worried expression, he smiled. "Just kidding. Winston is outside with the car."

"Thank you so much," Cynthia said as she stood up and extended her hand to Rebecca. "It has been a real honor to meet you—and thank you for the book! I will always treasure it."

"It's the least I could do," replied Rebecca. "I see great success for you in the future!"

CHAPTER 5

LESSON TWO: LEARNING FROM MISTAKES AND FAILURES

Outside the hotel, Winston was waiting by the car. Once Alex and Cynthia were safely inside, he took the wheel and the car glided away from the curb.

"That was amazing," said Cynthia to Alex. "I had heard so much about Rebecca Lowry, and to meet her and hear her advice has given me a huge boost of confidence. I'm sure it must be getting late—thank you, Alex, for a wonderful evening. I need to be getting back to the hotel."

"Late?" smiled Alex. "It's not late at all." He pointed out the window to a clock tower. "Do you see what time it is?"

"Yes," replied Cynthia. "It says nine o'clock. But that's impossible! We arrived at the Lowry Regency Hotel at nine o'clock. I remember seeing a clock behind the front desk."

Alex shrugged. "Time is a mysterious thing. Since it's still early, I think you can stay with the tour a little bit longer. Ah— we're at our next appointment!"

The car came to a stop in front of an office building. Winston opened the door and they stepped out.

On the sidewalk in front of the building was a huge statue of a teddy bear. Over the glass and chrome doors was a sign: WE ✦ TOYS.

"Don't tell me," said Cynthia, "but are you taking me to meet Peter Jordan? The legendary CEO of America's biggest toy retailer?"

"Okay, I won't tell you," replied Alex with a twinkle in his eye. "Let it be a surprise."

Sure enough, when the administrative assistant ushered them into the office of the CEO, from behind the big desk— which was covered with toys large and small—a jolly man greeted them with a booming voice: "Alex! Cynthia! Please come in! I've been expecting you!"

They took seats facing the desk. Without further introductions, Peter handed Cynthia a small ten-sided puzzle made of interlocking plastic pieces. "The goal is to move the pieces so that the numbers on them are lined up in order: 1-2-3-4-5-6-7-8-9-10."

"It looks simple enough," said Cynthia as she began manipulating the toy.

"Our field testing tells us the average fifth grader can do it in one minute," said Peter.

"Oh, now you're just trying to embarrass me!" retorted Cynthia. With a laugh she handed it back to Peter. "Let's see *you* do it!"

"I like you," said Peter. "You've got spunk!"

"I thought that since you have had a career that has been, shall we say, up and down," said Alex to Peter, "Cynthia would be most interested in hearing about how you've managed to overcome mistakes and failures to become the biggest toy retailer in the United States."

"Are you implying that my career has been nothing less than meteoric perfection?" laughed Peter. Putting aside a wind-up robot he had been fiddling with, he looked at Cynthia. "Of course, Alex is quite right. It's been a long hard road to get to where the company is today. I first got into the toy business after I graduated from college. I had a furniture store, and to fill up the shelves I added some toys. Soon I was selling more toys than furniture, so I got rid of the furniture. I renamed the store Jordan's Toy Emporium. But I didn't know anything about how to run a business, and we went bankrupt—not because we weren't good at selling toys, but because we tried to expand too fast and took on too much debt. That was a painful lesson! So I started over as WE ✦ TOYS. I built up the chain and went public. Another big mistake! During the last recession we were bought out by a holding company. Those guys didn't know anything about selling toys. I left the company and sailed a boat around the world. Then I got bored and, when the company was heading towards bankruptcy, I bought it back and took it private. Since then we've done pretty well—they call us a 'category killer.' We're dominating the market."

"I remember going to the first WE ✦ TOYS location when I was a kid," said Cynthia. "I loved it! It must have been hard to give it up and then start all over again."

"I learned a lot of lessons," replied Peter. "But they were good ones. I was lucky to have a mentor—my uncle Jack. He wasn't a rich man, but he knew a lot about how to keep a business going. Everything he taught me is right up here." He tapped his forehead. "And now I'm going to pass some of it along to you."

This is what he told Cynthia.

Why Leaders Fear Mistakes

Many leaders fear mistakes.

To be clear, there are some mistakes you *should* fear, because they can cost lives.

On February 1, 2003, the Space Shuttle Columbia disintegrated upon reentering Earth's atmosphere, killing all seven crew members. The cause? During the launch, a piece of foam insulation broke off from the main rocket's external tank and damaged the left wing of the orbiter. Upon re-entry ten days later, the damaged wing superheated, leading to the total loss of the craft. This was a very bad mistake—the kind no one wants to make.

Fortunately, in this book we're not talking about that kind

of mistake. We're talking about the mistakes that are made every day in business, and that if remedied can be relegated to the past.

In business, honest mistakes come in two basic varieties:

1. Human error during a standard, routine procedure. This is when a salesperson misplaces an order form, or when a fulfillment manager sends the wrong part.

These mistakes need to be quickly identified and corrected. If the *system* was the problem, it needs to be reviewed and possibly improved. If the *person* was the problem, the answer may be better training or, if the person just can't do the job, replacement.

2. An innovation that didn't work. These are the mistakes that many leaders fear. Risk scares them. The last thing they want is to spend money on a new idea only to have it fail. But such leaders don't realize that growth does not come without innovation, and innovation does not come without risk. You can never have progress without some mistakes being made along the way.

Many leaders fear mistakes because they can be expensive and they can lead to a loss of prestige. This is where *leadership* plays a key role. The tone is set at the top—and people in an organization need to know that mistakes should be quickly corrected, a review made, and then *you move ahead*.

You Cannot Grow Without Making Mistakes

Mistakes are valuable, because *growth* and *mistakes* go hand in hand. Just like a child learns to walk by getting up and falling down over and over again, a business can't grow without falling down a few times too.

Here are just two of the *benefits* of making mistakes.

1. Mistakes keep you focused and on your toes. As Bill Gates said, "Success is a lousy teacher. It seduces smart people into thinking they can't lose." There have been countless leaders who grew businesses during good times, or when there wasn't much competition, and who were blindsided when conditions became challenging. The best example of this syndrome is the arc of General Motors, America's—and once the world's—biggest automaker. Throughout the 1970s and 1980s, the company could do no wrong. General Motors built and sold the cars it assumed Americans wanted, and everyone involved in the company—leaders, unions, dealers—became (to put it bluntly) fat and happy. They ignored the rising challenge of Toyota and Volkswagen, who were making high quality, fuel-efficient vehicles. The moment of crisis came in 2009, when the Great Recession hit GM hard and forced the once invincible company into bankruptcy. Many experts and politicians urged the government to let it die.

But amazingly, there were a lot of good people at GM. With help from the US taxpayers, the company was given a second chance. A new leadership team changed the company culture and turned the company around. At the end of 2010, GM posted a profit of $4.7 billion—its first profitable year since 2004.

On January 15, 2014, Mary Barra was named CEO of the resurgent company—the first female CEO of a major global automaker. It's important to note that Barra was not an outside "gunslinger" who was brought into the company; she was a GM "lifer" who in 1980, at the age of eighteen, had started working for General Motors as a co-op student, and who had never worked anywhere else. (In fact her father, Ray Mäkelä, was another GM lifer, having worked as a die maker at Pontiac for thirty-nine years.)

Mary Barra had lived through all the mistakes made at GM—and they had taught her valuable lessons.

2. Mistakes are lessons that show you what doesn't work. Thomas Edison, America's greatest inventor, knew that his road to success was paved with mistakes. When searching for the right filament for his electric light, Edison is said to have made one thousand unsuccessful attempts. When a reporter asked, "How did it feel to fail a thousand times?" Edison replied, "I didn't fail a thousand times. The light bulb was an invention with a thousand steps."

He is also credited with saying, "I have not failed. I've just found ten thousand ways that won't work."

And also, "Many of life's failures are people who did not

realize how close they were to success when they gave up." (Thomas Edison is very quotable!)

Business leaders should put aside their fears and accept the value in making mistakes—as long as you learn from them. An honest culture allows people to take risks and be creative without fear of consequences.

As the nineteenth-century lawyer and diplomat Edward John Phelps said, "A man who makes no mistakes does not usually make anything."

Businesses that embrace error recognize the value in mistakes. They learn to make workable solutions and do something different.

A mistake isn't failure; it is a step closer to success!

Guidelines for Managing Mistakes

People make mistakes, and when a mistake is made people need to be either *commended* or *reprimanded*. Here are guidelines for how to make mistakes work for you, not against you.

1. Commend Good Mistakes

Good mistakes are the result of a desire to innovate and do a better job. They should be commended, analyzed, and then used as learning for the next step.

Bad mistakes are sloppy or lazy efforts, yielding poor results. Either fix the system or do a better job of training the employee.

2. Don't Make the Same Mistake Twice

When Thomas Edison tested one thousand filaments for his electric light, each test was of a different material. He never repeated a mistake! Don't tolerate the same mistake happening a second or third time. Repeated mistakes indicate that either the system is flawed or someone is not paying attention.

3. Kill Expensive Mistakes Quickly

If all mistakes turn into costly failures, they will soon bankrupt the company. The key is to kill or correct mistakes before they become disasters. For example, on August 2, 2016, Samsung unveiled the cutting-edge Galaxy Note 7 smartphone. The problem? Due to a design flaw, the battery had a habit of catching fire. Just one month later, Samsung suspended sales of the Galaxy Note 7. On October 11, the phone was pulled off the production line. The disaster had a major impact on Samsung's business in the third quarter of 2016, with the company projecting that its operating profits would be down by 33% in comparison to the previous quarter.

But Samsung moved quickly, and the improved Samsung Galaxy Note 8 was announced on August 23, 2017. This phone was a critical and marketplace success, and within six months the company had reportedly sold ten million units.

Every mistake is an opportunity in disguise!

How to Respond to Mistakes and Successes

Mistakes are a normal part of business. They're to be expected. The key to learning from mistakes and tipping the scales in the direction of successes is to engage the people responsible in two ways:

1. Respond Promptly

As soon as a mistake is identified, have a private one-on-one conversation with the person or people responsible. Don't enter the conversation with a judgment, no matter how obvious or egregious the mistake may be. Your first task is to gather information. So you would say, "Jim, I understand that the shipment of parts that was supposed to go to Mexico ended up in China. Can you tell me what happened?"

Then you *listen.*

Jim may either take responsibility for the mistake, or he may point to someone else or to a flaw in the system. If you're certain of what happened—if you know for a fact that Jim was sleeping at his desk and failed to respond to the correct shipping instructions—then you can ask Jim how you can help him stay awake and avoid future mistakes. Did he fall asleep because he has a newborn baby at home and he was up at three o'clock in the morning? Or did he fall asleep because he was out late with his buddies?

Would a change in Jim's work schedule help him? Or is this a problem he needs to solve on his own?

The key is that the problem should be addressed immediately. Jim deserves to know where he stands and how he can do better. Do not wait until the annual performance review. By then it's too late. Annual performance reviews are valuable only to determine if someone is getting a raise or a promotion. That's it. They are a horrible way to rehash past mistakes that should have been resolved long ago.

2. Respond With Clarity

By definition, a mistake is when you do something that's not in accordance with an established system. It's when you cook the French fries for two minutes instead of three minutes. It's when you write the wrong account number on an order form. It's when you're late filing a legal document with the court, and your case gets thrown out.

People who have made mistakes can't improve their performance without having a clear goal.

It's terrible to say to an employee, "Do better next time!" Or, "Next time be more careful!" What do those instructions mean? Nobody knows.

It's important that the employee knows what's expected. If there's a problem, it may be that the employee just isn't capable of doing the job, or that he or she hasn't been trained properly. If training is the issue, as a leader that's your responsibility.

Praise Successes Promptly

Just as mistakes need to be dealt with quickly, praise should be delivered promptly as well. Numerous studies have shown that employees are most motivated by praise from colleagues and superiors. In fact, it's more effective than cash bonuses. But it has to come in real time. For example, let's say Cynthia receives a report that the soybean division of Conglomerated landed a big new contract with a food manufacturer. She would immediately pick up the phone and congratulate the people responsible and say, "Job well done!" She would not wait until an executive team meeting later in the week. She would not wait until the annual performance review, by which time it would be ancient history.

Praise and constructive criticism are both best served piping hot, fresh off the stove!

CHAPTER 6

LESSON THREE: UNDERSTAND YOUR STORY

When they had returned to the waiting Rolls-Royce, Cynthia said to Alex, "That was an incredible experience! It was amazing to see Peter's infectious optimism. He really seems to love what he does, and I can see why he could suffer business reversals and bounce back stronger than before. It's all a matter of your attitude. If you see a mistake as representing a crushing defeat, or as evidence of a personal flaw, then you'll be mired in negativity. But if you see a mistake as a learning experience, then you'll move forward with even more energy." She glanced out the tinted window at the passing cityscape. "I don't see a clock… but I'll bet it's still nine o'clock! Thank you so much, Alex, for what you've shown me. I'm sure you need to get back."

"I'm in no hurry," smiled Alex. "The night is still young!"

Winston expertly brought the car to a stop in front of a big brick building that looked like a nineteenth-century warehouse. The tall windows had been bricked in. There was a door with a small sign that read "MADELINE STUDIOS."

Alex knocked on the door, and after a few moments a young man answered. He was wearing a black t-shirt and jeans.

"Alex Tomlin to see Karen Madeline," said Alex.

Without a word the young man waved them inside. He took them to an old-fashioned elevator, the kind used in factories and warehouses. Despite the building's age, Cynthia noted the wooden floors were spotless and the lighting fixtures were expensive. On the exposed brick walls were hung movie posters in thin gold frames.

The elevator door lurched open and the young man led them to an office door marked EDITING. He knocked. A woman's voice bade them enter.

Cynthia found herself in a room filled with video and film editing equipment. A woman was peering into a small viewer. After a moment she said to the man next to her, "That's it. Right there. In this scene we're going to cut from the farmhouse to the farmer in the field. Do you think we should do a cross dissolve from the house to the farmer, or a fade?"

"A cross dissolve," replied the man.

"Okay. Let's do that." Then she looked up. "Why hello, Alex!" she said cheerily. She extended her hand to Cynthia. "I'm Karen. It's a pleasure to meet you. Please—we can talk over here." She motioned to what looked like a little lounge area furnished with an oriental rug, a table and chairs, and a vintage sofa.

"I've heard so much about you," said Cynthia as they sat down at the table. "And your last film—*Ruby's Song*—was really extraordinary. The ending brought me to tears."

"You're very kind," replied Karen. "Alex tells me you're the new CEO of Conglomerated Industries. Congratulations! The company has a fascinating story. Elijah Paulson was a true pioneer in how he built the business from that one decrepit grain silo he inherited from his uncle in 1920. But from the tiny acorn grows the great oak!"

"Yes, and now the mighty tree has many branches—but unfortunately some are not as healthy as others," replied Cynthia.

"Judicious pruning might be in order," said Alex.

"In this room we edit our films," replied Karen. "That often means leaving on the cutting room floor some lovely scenes." She shrugged. "You have to do what's best for the film. You can't become sentimental about a shot that doesn't work." She looked at Cynthia. "Alex told me that you're very bright and hard working. I'm sure you'll be a great success! I know that no one who succeeds does so on their own. I was helped by many people who gave me advice and opportunities along the way, and I'm very happy to help you in any way I can."

"I was hoping that perhaps you could give Cynthia some insight into the importance of understanding your story," said

Alex.

"I've heard that expression, but I'm not sure what it means," said Cynthia.

"Good!" Karen smiled and slapped her hand on the table.

"Is it good that I don't know?" asked Cynthia.

"It's good that you're willing to *say*, 'I don't know,'" replied Karen. "It means you're honest and you don't care about putting up a false front. You're willing to seek advice. That's very important. Alex is right. You should understand your story—and by that I mean both your personal story and your company's story."

Here's what Karen told Cynthia.

Your Personal Story as a Leader: Crossroads Moments

It's difficult to be a confident leader if you don't have a strong sense of self identity. The challenge is to make the transition from being the hero of your own journeys to an authentic leader who empowers others.

What matters most are your transformative experiences. I call them *crossroads moments*, and they come when you are faced with difficult choices. They may happen at any point in your life. A crossroads moment could be positive, such as when you were offered an opportunity and you chose to seize it. (It's amazing how many people *avoid* seizing opportunities because they lack confidence!) A crossroads moment could be a big challenge, such as a business setback, an illness, or some sort of disaster.

Your crossroads moment takes you to the core of your being and compels you to look at yourself, closely examine your values and your character, and fully recognize who you are. Even if you do not recognize its importance when you're in the middle of the experience, when seen in retrospect, your crossroads moment may represent a defining experience in your life.

Having passed through the crossroads moment, or reflecting on it later with the benefit of hindsight, you'll see the world differently, and this new knowledge will shape your decisions. It is during such a transition that you'll realize effective leadership is not primarily about getting others to follow you or becoming personally enriched. Instead, you understand that the essence of leadership is aligning your teammates around a shared vision and values, and empowering them to step up and take responsibility.

The crossroads moment can help you change your viewpoint from "me" to "we."

The transformation from "me" to "we" forces you to be humble. This newly found humility stems from the recognition that leadership is not just about you. It's related to the ancient concept of servant leadership, which appears in the *Tao Te Ching*, attributed to Lao-Tzu, who is believed to have lived in China sometime between 570 BCE and 490 BCE:

> The highest type of ruler is one of whose existence the people are barely aware.

Next comes one whom they love and praise.

Next comes one whom they fear.

Next comes one whom they despise and defy.

When you are lacking in faith,

Others will be unfaithful to you.

The Sage is self-effacing and scanty of words.

When his task is accomplished and things have been completed, all the people say, "We ourselves have achieved it!"

This is the true essence of leadership.

The other story you need to know and understand is the story of your organization.

The Stories of Your Company

Great leaders are often great storytellers.

I mean this literally. They know how to convey a story to an audience that will help them to understand something better. Leaders can frame their companies' core narratives to connect authentically with different audiences.

The first step to becoming a powerful storytelling leader is to understand and master what Carol Barash in *Entrepreneur Magazine* called the three key stories about your company: the numbers story, the vision story, and the bridge story.

1. The Numbers Story

This is exactly what it sounds like. You need to be able to

take a bunch of numbers, such as key performance indicators, and give them context. Weave them into a story that makes sense. I don't mean it should be a fairy tale or something grandiose. It needs to be a narrative that inspires your people to get engaged and committed to reaching their goals (which may be represented by numbers!). Facts and figures and all the dry things that we think are important in the business world don't stick in our minds very well. But stories create "sticky" memories by attaching emotions to information tied to business performance.

Good storytellers know that a story needs a source of conflict. Is there a market challenge that needs to be overcome? A competitor who needs to be bested? If you say that the company's sales are down by five percent, what's the context—is it due to a bad economy, outdated products, or an ineffective sales strategy?

Don't hesitate to suggest the road ahead will be tough. People like to be told the challenge will be difficult. Visionary leaders say to their employees, "This is going to be difficult. But if we all work together and don't give up, in the end we'll achieve something positive."

Don't load up your story with needless details that detract from your core message. "Key performance indicators" are given that name because they're *key*—which means that other data is going to be irrelevant to your audience. Work from the principle that "less is more." One of the biggest mistakes you can make is putting in too much detail that will serve to only confuse and frustrate your listeners.

2. The Vision Story

As the name implies, the vision story has nothing to do with key performance indicators or numbers. It's all about the purpose and mission of the company, and what each member of the organization can contribute.

You'll recall the Conglomerated board meeting when Ruth Paulson, the great-granddaughter of Elijah Paulson, reminded the board members that her great-grandfather had started the business to feed his neighbors and build safe houses for them. To her, this was the story of Conglomerated Industries, and one in which she took great pride.

The vision story is the intersection of the past—where the company has been—and the future. The leader takes the audience to the future by making it true in the present. The vision story is bigger than simply projecting business outcomes and much more compelling than goal setting. The vision story is the story you tell employees, investors, advisors, and yourself to generate creativity and belief in the present.

This is not to say that the vision story can't represent a change in direction from the past. Often, this is when it's most important. For example, consider the National Geographic Society, which published its first magazine in 1888. The familiar yellow-bound journal became a household staple for generations of American families. But times changed, and in the 1990s the magazine started to shed subscribers as younger readers abandoned it for the internet.

National Geographic Society CEO John Fahey didn't wait for his publication to decline into bankruptcy like so many other print magazines. Instead, he spearheaded a strategy to reinvent the National Geographic brand across all media platforms, and especially with the National Geographic Channel, launched in 2001.

"We have always been a brand that has stood with science and the facts," National Geographic Partners chief marketing officer Jill Cress told CMO.com. "There is a ton of science around climate and what's happening. We've started a dialogue around that." The core story of the company hasn't really changed at all—only how it's being delivered.

3. The Bridge Story

Every company has a story to tell that will connect potential customers to your brand. The most powerful, persuasive communication has a human element effectively delivered through stories. The bridge story makes the vision story real for your audience by citing past successes as proof that the vision is attainable. It's where you connect what the business has done in the past and where you will take it in the future.

The "a-ha moment," popularized by Oprah Winfrey, is the point in a story when an audience learns the value proposition of the product or service. As she told Merriam-Webster, "I always love those moments when I sit down to talk to somebody and they say something that makes me look at life or a situation in a completely different way. And I say, 'A-ha! I get it!' Light bulb! Bing, bing, bing moment. And the little hairs on your arm stand up. That is an 'a-ha moment.'"

Remember, the organizational story is iterative and evolutionary. It's not one story for all time, but rather a river of interpretation and reinterpretation according to circumstance and situation. Stories change over time, with each one written according to the latest synergy between past, present, and future.

CHAPTER 7

LESSON FOUR: BUILDING COALITIONS

"Three valuable life lessons in the blink of an eye!" exclaimed Cynthia as the Rolls-Royce pulled away from the curb outside Madeleine Studios. "I'm already beginning to feel more confident."

"Can I tell you a secret?" said Alex. "You've always been confident. You're the same person now as you were when you first stepped into this car. The only difference is that you're beginning to give yourself permission to *show* and *act on* your confidence. But that's okay—it's a trait of human nature to seek validation. That's what experienced mentors can give you. They teach you how to think." He leaned forward to speak to Winston. "See that office building on the next block? That's the one."

The car glided to a stop, and Winston opened the doors. Cynthia, who by now knew what to look for, scanned the gleaming glass entranceway. Over the door, in gold script, was one name: "Overton's."

"Is this *the* Overton's?" asked Cynthia as they approached the doors. "It's one of the most legendary cosmetics companies in America!"

"Yes, this is the one," smiled Alex as they pushed through the revolving doors into the marble-floored lobby. The elevator whisked them to executive suite, and a moment later they were ushered into an office.

"Joanne Overton, I'd like you to meet Cynthia Langford," said Alex as a woman looked up from a sack of color swatches she was examining.

Joanne smiled. "Please sit down." Cynthia took her seat, but couldn't help twisting around to look at all the framed photographs hanging on the walls that showed Joanne with nationally known celebrities.

"Ah—my little gallery," laughed Joanne. "In my business, you have to get to know people. You need to spend time with them. Cosmetics is very personal. It's one-on-one. I still give makeup clinics to our customers. I guess you could say I'm the number one brand ambassador."

"That also applies to how you operate internally as well," offered Alex. "You're known to be a very hands-on leader."

"Well, let's just say that when I became CEO, there were some divisions within the company—which, like Conglomerated Industries, is family owned. We had some bridges to mend. I realized that if you want to build bridges, you've got to get out of your office and go into the world. You've got to pick up a hammer and a saw and get to work. You need to reach out to people whom you might not want to touch with a ten-foot pole!" She laughed. "But you know what? I'm sure that there were people in my own company who had misconceptions about me. When I was first appointed CEO, there were articles in the paper that said I was nothing but a party girl, and who was I to lead Overton's? I knew these stories weren't true, but it was up to me to get out there, meet people, and show them I was ready to lead this great company. One by one, I won them over. One by one. That's what it takes."

"Almost like being a politician," said Cynthia.

"Yes," replied Joanne. "You know, many leaders think that just because they have a fancy title on the door, their employees need to jump whenever they snap their fingers. Nothing could be further from the truth. Your employees need to respect you, and respect must be *earned*. It doesn't happen by magic. It doesn't happen by wishful thinking. And it certainly won't happen if you shut yourself up in your office and issue memos."

"I know what you mean," said Cynthia. "I've heard through the grapevine that my predecessor wasn't well respected. This was not because he was a bad person—in fact, everyone who knows him says he's a very nice man who treats people well. But he didn't get out of the office. He *assumed* that because he was a nice person, everyone would perceive him that way. This allowed people who disagreed with him to gossip and tell stories about him, and he wasn't there to show them otherwise.

Eventually he lost control of the company and the board voted him out."

"And you don't want to make the same mistake," said Joanne.

"No. And besides, I like to think that I'm naturally gregarious. I like getting out of the office. I like to 'manage by wandering around,' as the saying goes."

"And let's be honest," said Joanne. "A leader needs to build coalitions. You need to know who's backing you and who might be adversarial. That's just a fact of life, especially with a board of directors, who decide important issues by majority shareholder vote. To get anything done, you need that fifty-one percent of the shares behind you. Hopefully more—but at least a majority!"

Change Begins With Board Support

The essence of growth and success in business is *change.* It comes in two forms:

1. The introduction of new ideas. These can be new products, new business relationships, new ways of managing, or the use of a new technology.

2. The elimination of old ideas that aren't working. As is the case with #1, this can include products, business relationships, management practices, technology— anything that impacts the company's ability to carry out its mission and serve its customers.

Both forms of change are equally important.

Many components play a key role in successful change, and your biggest driving force will always be *people*. People will ultimately push your idea over the top, whether it be through policy implementation, advocacy, personal connections, funding, market knowledge, influence, or simply word of mouth.

People can either embrace a new idea or reject it.

People can either agree to discard an old method or, if they're personally threatened by such a change, can fight it tooth and nail.

If you're in a leadership position like Cynthia, where a strong board of directors sets the organization's agenda and needs to approve any significant changes to the company or its mission, the first set of people you need to back you are the members of the board. They hold the keys to either unlock progress or stifle it.

The fact that you may have the title "CEO" and a big office may be irrelevant to how the board members view what you want to do. After all, you're their employee! What's worse, in a meeting they may smile in agreement to your face before going back to their regular lives vowing to never lift a finger to help you implement what they just agreed to.

That's why you need to build strong coalitions.

A coalition is an alliance of groups or individuals in order to achieve a common purpose or to engage in joint activity. Coalition building is the process by which parties come together to form a common interest group. Forming coalitions with other people and groups of similar values, interests, and goals allows members to combine their resources and become more powerful than when they each acted alone.

Generally, people form a coalition from a position of relative weakness—that is, individually they are not strong enough in the organization to achieve their goals.

Building coalitions is imperative to success because you need early adoption and advocacy of new ideas. If you wait until the final steps of development to seek these relationships, you will find yourself behind the curve. Without coalitions, you have to forge ahead alone—and that's a lonely place to be.

Building a successful coalition involves a series of steps. The steps begin with the recognition of compatible interests. Sometimes this happens easily, while other times potential coalition members must be persuaded that forming a coalition would be to their benefit. To do this you need to demonstrate these three realities:

1. Your goals are similar and compatible. For instance, at Conglomerated Industries Cynthia needs to make sure it's a common goal among all the board members that the company grow, be profitable, and remain independent. It's possible that some board members want to sell the company, and all they care about is devising an exit strategy, while others might want to raise capital by taking the company public. These are fundamental issues that Cynthia needs to explore, and she can do that only by engaging the board members one on one.

2. Working together will enhance both groups' abilities to reach their goals. This is a recognition of the fact that since no one at Conglomerated owns a majority of the company, any measure that needs board approval requires a coalition. But this is also important for everyday company operations. For example, a new product initiative must have active support from every stakeholder involved. Sometimes a leader can simply announce, "This is what we're doing," and people will respond; but it's much smarter to bring people onboard by showing them why the new idea is good and getting them fully engaged.

3. The benefits of unity are greater than the costs. There is an element of the carrot and the stick. The carrot is the benefit. The stick is the price you pay for not getting on board. A leader can explain why a new idea is a good one, and he or she can also explain how inaction, or some other solution that isn't favored, will harm the company and its employees.

In addition, a coalition can bring more expertise and resources to bear on a complex issue where the knowledge base of any one person is insufficient. For example, if Cynthia were to seek to sell off the Mega Wet World division, she might be challenged by Aretha, who could say, "Well, you have no expertise in the family water park business, so how would you know what to do?" If Cynthia had on her team someone with experience in the industry, she'd have more credibility.

In addition, as another benefit each member of the coalition is more likely to gain access to the contacts and relationships established by other members. It's like being a member of a club, where personal familiarity brings more comfort with resource sharing.

Maintain Relationships

Especially if you're a newcomer to an organization that is well entrenched and has a long history, like Cynthia joining Conglomerated, you need to build up trust with everyone with whom you work—your superiors, your colleagues, and your employees. You need to learn whom you can trust, and you need to demonstrate to others—even those opposed to you— that they can trust you.

This cannot happen quickly. It takes time. Above all, it takes *repeated tests*. Trust is built one transaction at a time. You can't afford to break your word even once.

Let's say—hypothetically—that before one of Cynthia's first board meetings, Aretha approaches Cynthia and says, "I'm going to talk about Mega Wet World at the meeting, and I need the most current financials, which I've been told reflect a profit for this quarter. Please make sure I have them—I need to share some good news about this troubled subsidiary."

Cynthia agrees, not just because it's her job to provide that type of information to board members, but because she's a fair-minded person who wants everyone to know the facts.

But Cynthia also knows that many board members want to sell Mega Wet World, and are annoyed that Aretha keeps promoting what they think is a losing venture. They don't even want to hear good news about it.

If Cynthia fails to deliver the positive financials to Aretha before the meeting, or worse yet skews them to seem negative (numbers can be fudged!), then she will permanently alienate Aretha, who will never trust her again. Not a big problem? It could be a huge problem for Cynthia if in the future she needs Aretha's support on another issue.

As Aretha will say, "What goes around, comes around."

No one likes to feel used. If you enlist the support of various individuals to accomplish a goal, keep your promises. A month later, don't pretend you don't know them. Maintain the relationship by keeping everyone informed of its progress. Be sure to thank your supporters publicly (if appropriate). Include them in future deliberations—they may share a common view in other areas as well.

CHAPTER 8

LESSON FIVE: GREAT CUSTOMER SERVICE

At exactly nine o'clock that night—it was always nine o'clock!—the Rolls-Royce Silver Spirit eased to a stop in front of a downtown business hotel.

"Another hotel CEO?" asked Cynthia as she alighted from the car.

"No," replied Alex as they made their way through the busy lobby and up an escalator. "You'll see."

They went into one of the hotel conference rooms, where there were people in business attire milling about. Cynthia noticed that the women wore styles she remembered from the late nineteen eighties. With the men, you couldn't tell much difference, except the shoulder pads seemed bigger and the hair was longer. Thankfully, no one was wearing parachute pants.

Cynthia was glad she had worn a dress with a classically tailored look—good taste, she reminded herself, never goes out of style.

At the head of the room was a plain table, some chairs behind it, and a podium. Some men and women were there. They seemed like they were presenters.

After they put on the ubiquitous adhesive name tags ("Hello! My name is Cynthia "), Alex headed straight for the head table, with Cynthia following.

A man turned to them. "Why, hello, Alex!" He then extended his hand to Cynthia. "I'm Jim Banning. It's a pleasure to meet you."

"Oh, now I recognize you," said Cynthia. "You're the founder and CEO of Express Airways, the airline that's shaking up the industry with your emphasis on customer service."

"That's right," replied Jim. "And that's why we're here tonight. This is our Chicago Industrial Association roundtable on—you guessed it—customer service!"

"Jim," said Alex, "you know as well as I do that today in the airline industry, 'customer service' is almost a dirty word. At most airlines, passengers are treated like cattle. They're squeezed into tiny seats and all they get to eat is a crummy little packet of sticky peanuts."

"That's exactly why Express Airlines stock is leading the pack on Wall Street," replied Jim. "I started the airline because I saw an opportunity. I knew we could provide much better customer service than the big guys and still keep our prices competitive. Our shareholders agree."

"What's the number one secret of great customer service?"

asked Cynthia.

"In my opinion—and I'm sure you'll hear other viewpoints here tonight—the most critical element is your people. Nothing is more important than the interactions between your representatives and your customers. Let me put it to you this way. When someone buys a ticket on Express Airlines, they know they're going to be flying in a very basic aircraft. We're an economy airline and that's what our customers want. No frills. But what makes the experience pleasant and non-stressful is how we treat our customers. From the moment they call our 800 number and get a real person on the line, to the ticket agent at the airport, the flight attendants, how their baggage is handled—all of it must be seamless and happy. And it is."

"How do you achieve this?" asked Cynthia. "Do you have massive training programs?"

"Yes, we do," replied Jim, "but that's the least important part. The key is in our hiring."

"Hiring?"

"Yes! We believe that you can't teach someone to be nice. We can teach our new hires job skills, like how to use a ticket machine, but we can't change someone's personality. When we hire, we look very carefully at the person and how they interact with our people. They have to have a fundamental desire to please other people, even under difficult circumstances. Only after we're convinced they have what it takes do we hire them.

"We follow the adage, 'Hire slow, fire fast.' Every person we hire—even the mechanics who never interact with customers—

are hired on a probationary basis. After being on the job for two weeks, we offer them a lump sum of money to quit. We say, 'We'll pay you to leave if you're not totally committed.' A few of them do this. And you know what? By taking the cash, they save us money! Do you know how much one unhappy customer can cost a business in lost sales? Or the cost of an employee who isn't engaged, or who's chronically late? We've found that it's better for both parties if the unhappy employee leaves quickly."

"This is all about fitting in with the company culture, isn't it?" asked Cynthia.

"Exactly! In the hiring process, cultural fit is one of the most important selection criterion. An employee who doesn't mesh with our culture will negatively affect those around them. They can stifle the dynamics, motivation, and enthusiasm of their team. Poor employee motivation can diminish the productivity—and profitability—of our organization."

Jim told Cynthia that great customer service is important for two other reasons:

1. You want repeat customers. You want the lifetime value of each customer to be high. As every businessperson knows, the cost of acquiring a new customer is much higher than the cost of servicing an existing customer. You don't create a lifetime customer unless he or she has a consistently positive experience, time after time.

2. Happy customers are brand ambassadors. Jim said to Cynthia, "Do you know what happens when Christine gets back to the office after her Caribbean vacation? Her coworkers ask her if she had a good time. They ask her what hotel she stayed at, and what airline she used. We want Christine to say she flew Express Airlines and it was perfectly fine. No problems. Very pleasant flight. We do not want her reporting we lost her luggage or the plane was delayed or the flight attendant was rude. Then all of her coworkers will hear this, and we'll lose a dozen prospective customers. Not good!"

Building Great Customer Service

Cynthia told Jim that because Conglomerated was primarily a business-to-business (B2B) company (there were a few exceptions, including Mega Wet World and the Little Miss Paulson snack foods), the company didn't have much institutional experience with retail customers. But she felt that in the near future Conglomerated would need to get into the business-to-consumer (B2C) space, and customer service would become a priority.

He replied that it should be a priority *now*, even with their corporate customers. "A customer is a customer," he said. "The only difference is scale. You might have one customer—a buyer for a food manufacturer, say—who buys ten million dollars worth of corn meal. Or you might have ten million retail customers, and each one buys a Little Miss Paulson snack cake for one dollar. Either way it's ten million dollars."

Probably the biggest difference between selling B2B and selling B2C is the use of digital social media. If you've only sold B2B, you may be forgiven for being clueless about the power of Twitter, Instagram, Facebook, and Angie's List. These are the spaces where consumer tastes are shaped, and woe to the company—including Mega Wet World—that doesn't understand how much consumers rely on their phones to get information about products or services they want to buy.

Cynthia made a mental note that once she returned to the twenty-first century, she needed to check on Mega Wet World's online presence. If it were weak—or even non-existent—the company would be operating at a huge disadvantage to its rivals with strong digital platforms. Hiring a director of digital media to report directly to the marketing director would be mandatory.

Whether you're selling to companies or consumers, your goal should always be to make your customer happy. For example, when online retailer Zappos shifted their focus from selling shoes to pleasing customers, their employees became more engaged, customers were happier, and sales skyrocketed.

There's a big difference between trying to *sell* something to somebody and trying to *make them happy*. When you're focused on making the customer happy, you start to understand the complete customer experience, and how making a sale becomes a natural outcome of a positive experience.

Customer Touch Points

The customer's journey from prospect to a repeat customer is characterized by a series of *touch points*. Each touch point must result in a happy customer. Touch points can be different for every company and even every product, but here is a representative sample:

1. Awareness. The consumer becomes aware of your product or service. This is critical with a new product, but established products can fade from consumer consciousness and need to be re-introduced.

2. Interest. Now the consumer is considering buying your product. They may visit your website to learn more about it, or even order it with the guarantee they can send it back.

3. Purchase. The consumer pays—but the game is not over because consumers have rights to return just about anything for a refund or credit.

4. Use. Now the consumer is using the product. It needs to meet or exceed his or her expectations.

5. Communication. Many consumers post reviews or comments online, or they tell their friends. They may also have a problem that needs to be quickly solved by the company.

6. Repeat. This is what you want: Your customer to feel comfortable to buy again and again, even without "shopping around" or checking the competition. This is brand loyalty. It's very powerful and very valuable!

When measuring the effectiveness of each of your customer

touch points, be sure you don't miss the forest for the trees. By this we mean you can have success at every touch point and still lose the customer. How can this happen? If there are too many touch points and the journey is too complicated, you can have customer fatigue.

For example, Cynthia discovered that customers visiting Mega Wet World had to endure too many interactions before being free to enjoy the park. They had to pay to park, then pay to enter, then get a locker, then buy passes.... by the time they got into the water, they were exhausted! Most of their encounters with staff were positive in a narrow sense, but the cumulative effect on customer experience was burdensome, and many customers never came back.

At the heart of the problem was the siloed nature of the company's service delivery. There was no one person in charge of the customer experience, and each functional area, from the people who operated the website to the manager of the parking lot, designed its own set of customer interactions. No one was looking at the big picture.

Take the time and effort to look at your touch points as not just isolated, singular experiences, but as a collective whole. This will help you shape them for a better customer experience, and perhaps even point to opportunities to either invent new types of touch points or eliminate ones that aren't necessary.

Be sure to consider the impact of third party partners who may be handling your customers for you. For example, in the 1990s Apple became dissatisfied with retailers, including the now-defunct CompUSA, who were not doing a good enough job demonstrating the Mac experience. In response, in 2001 Apple began building its own stores. At the time, most analysts thought that Apple's move was a crazy idea. Today Apple stores are considered retail icons and a key reason why Apple has been able to attract a very broad audience.

Be sure to put yourself in your customer's shoes! Would *you* want to buy from your company?

CHAPTER 9

LESSON SIX: CONCENTRATION AND FOCUS

The Rolls-Royce sighed to a stop outside a restaurant with a sign over the sidewalk that simply said "Joe's."

Alex and Cynthia went inside.

"Say, I've heard of this place," said Cynthia as they were seated at a booth. "This is the legendary Joe's Seafood, Prime Steak & Stone Crab. It's one of the most well-known restaurants in Chicago!"

"Yes, it's a local landmark," replied Alex. "And even though it's only nine o'clock, and according to the clock we've just finished dinner at The Berghoff, I'll bet you're famished."

"Now that you mention it, I am rather hungry," replied Cynthia.

"That's because your stomach thinks it's after midnight. In

my special limousine service I have a limited number of tricks up my sleeve—holding back hunger pangs isn't one of them!" Alex saw a man approaching the booth. "Ah—our special guest has arrived!"

Cynthia looked up from her menu.

"Patrick Stevens, meet Cynthia Langford," said Alex as the man slid into the booth.

"Oh, my gosh," sputtered Cynthia as she extended her hand. "I've seen you many times on television. On PBS they broadcast your personal development seminars late at night. I'm always awake and I love to watch them!"

"Do you have difficulty sleeping?" asked Patrick. His sharp eyes seemed to drill into hers.

"I often have a lot on my mind," replied Cynthia. Embarrassed, she looked down at her menu.

"You've just become the CEO of one of the biggest privately held companies in the United States," replied Patrick. "You're to be congratulated. I'm sure it was a long hard climb."

"In fact, it was," said Cynthia.

"I invited Patrick to join us," said Alex, "because as one of America's most prominent personal development and business leadership gurus, he's uniquely positioned to offer you some advice."

"I hardly expect a free consultation," said Cynthia. "I'd be happy to pay your normal fee."

"Don't be concerned," replied Patrick with a wave of his hand. "My price is dinner from my friend Alex!"

"Agreed!" said Alex. He leaned forward and looked Cynthia in the eye. "You've gotten very good advice tonight from some of the living legends of business. I know you'll put it to good use. Tonight I'd like to talk to you about something that can make a big difference in every part of your life, not just your business—although it will definitely help you in your career. I want to talk about concentration and focus, both in your role as CEO and for the company itself."

"Both of us could use some," admitted Cynthia. "Being the leader of a company as diverse as Conglomerated means I'm thinking about ten different things at once. It's enough to give you whiplash! And the business lines of Conglomerated Industries are very diverse. Sometimes I wonder exactly what our direction should be."

"I understand," said Patrick. "The answer cannot be, 'We do anything that makes money.' That's exactly the wrong approach!"

The Company Mission Statement

Patrick reviewed with Cynthia the importance of the company's mission statement. He showed her some outstanding mission statements from successful companies. They included:

Casper mattresses: "Great sleep, made simple."

Facebook: "Founded in 2004, Facebook's mission is to give people the power to build community and bring the world closer together. People use Facebook to stay connected with friends and family, to discover what's going on in the world, and to share and express what matters to them."

Google: "Google's mission is to organize the world's information and make it universally accessible and useful."

Starbucks: "To inspire and nurture the human spirit—one person, one cup, and one neighborhood at a time."

Tesla: "Our goal when we created Tesla a decade ago was the same as it is today: to accelerate the advent of sustainable transport by bringing compelling mass market electric cars to market as soon as possible."

General Electric: "To invent the next industrial era, to build, move, power and cure the world."

Every organization needs a mission statement. It serves as your GPS system, to keep you on track as you journey through unfamiliar territory.

But why adopt a mantra that you might say is limiting? Why not just say, "We can be great at whatever we do"?

Because human beings can't be great at everything. Not even Leonardo da Vinci, who was probably the most multitalented human being who ever lived, wasn't great at *everything*. He had his areas of expertise. People function best when they develop a particular skill and hone it. Organizations work best when they're comprised of people who possess related and complementary skills. For example, in a successful automobile company the engineers, the marketing people, the workers on the assembly line, and the finance people all have different skill sets, but they're united by their interest in building and selling cars. They're not interested in selling shoes or hamburgers or laundry soap. They like cars, and that's what they do.

Cynthia mentioned to Patrick that she had briefly discussed the Conglomerated mission statement with Rebecca Lowry, and that Rebecca had commented it was overly long and vague. Patrick nodded.

Sooner or later, the subject of the company's mission statement had to be addressed. But how?

Very carefully, very openly, and step by step.

The first thing Cynthia needed to do was get Mr. Paulson, the chairman of the board, to get behind the idea of rewriting the company's mission statement. This should be done slowly and discreetly, by first educating Mr. Paulson on the importance of a clear and inspiring mission statement. Once he was on board, Cynthia would then work with Mr. Paulson to form a coalition of board members who also backed the idea. The key thing is that at this stage you're *not* saying what the new mission statement should be, only that the old one needs to be clarified. The new mission statement will be written only after receiving input from a wide range of stakeholders, including front line employees.

Once a majority coalition has been formed, only then should the idea be introduced openly to the board.

(This leads us to the Golden Rule of running board meetings: NO SURPRISES. The majority of board members should always be aware of an issue, and support it, *before* it's formally introduced at a meeting. An issue that does not have majority support should never be taken up.)

Once the board approves the idea of revising the mission statement, then you name a committee. They are charged with crafting a carefully orchestrated series of town halls and stakeholder surveys to collect opinions and ideas, and write up a report for the board.

Then the board votes, and the new mission statement is approved.

Is the mission statement then carved in stone over the front door of the company headquarters, and expected to last forever?

Or perhaps even worse, shoved into the back of a drawer, never to be seen again?

No. The mission statement is like your GPS. When you begin a long journey, you don't just look at it once and then turn off your phone. You keep it in front of you, in plain sight. And if for some reason you want to deliberately change your route or destination, you can re-program your GPS to keep you headed where you want to go.

Successful companies know they want to *make the lives of their customers better*. That should always be their concentration and focus.

Your Personal Mission Statement

Patrick explained to Cynthia that just as organizations need mission statements, so do leaders.

You can call it whatever you want—your purpose, your goal in life, or "what gets me out of bed in the morning." Your mission could be as simple as wanting to raise your kids to be happy and healthy—there's nothing wrong with that! If you're a soldier, your mission might be to defend and protect your country.

Or your mission could be your vocation—to be the very best leader or team member of an organization that does something you think is worthwhile and you believe in. This is what Patrick wanted to talk to Cynthia about. What was her personal mission—her concentration and focus—as she approached her new tenure as CEO of Conglomerated?

"I don't know," replied Cynthia. "I never really thought about it. I just aimed for the next promotion. That was my focus—to get promoted."

"Well, now you're the CEO of a global corporation," replied Patrick with a smile. "No more promotions! So what do you want to do?"

"I guess the first thing I want to do is not mess up!" said Cynthia. They laughed.

"Actually, that's not a bad answer," said Patrick. "The Hippocratic oath for physicians says, 'First do no harm.' The same rule applies to powerful leaders."

Patrick explained that living your life according to your personal mission statement helps you stay focused on what's important to you. Once you formulate your mission statement, you begin living it. By setting clear boundaries, it becomes an important tool for making tough decisions. It frees your mind and your energy to concentrate on what matters to you.

Formulating your own mission statement can seem like a daunting task. But like any other job, if you take it one step at a time it's not so difficult.

A good way to do it is to ask yourself a series of five questions. Your answers need not be lengthy—in fact, shorter is probably better.

The Five Questions

1. What is important to me? Your answer should not be a material thing, like "having more money than anyone else." While having money can be an extremely important goal if you're currently facing eviction because you can't pay your rent, it's a fact of life that you can make money doing just about anything. Money is a natural outcome of doing something really well and providing value to people.

Do you know who John Ades was? He was a resident of New York City who made a very comfortable living selling potato peelers on the street. From 1993 until his death in 2009, Ades sold $5 metal potato peelers to passers-by. He sold enough peelers to enjoy café society at the Pierre Hotel, on the Upper East Side, and live with his wife in their three-bedroom apartment on Park Avenue. John Ades was a man who had focus and concentration!

At the other end of the spectrum is Elon Musk. As this

visionary engineer and entrepreneur told TheHenryFord.org in 2009, "The reason I'm doing SpaceX is not due to some childhood epiphany or because I think this is the highest return on your investment or a way to spend money. I think starting a rocket company is an unusual thing to do and pretty risky. But I'm a big believer in us becoming a space exploring civilization and, ultimately, extending life beyond earth. When I was in college I tried to think what are the really big problems that face the world, which will most affect the future of humanity? And the three that I thought were the most important were the Internet, transition to a sustainable energy economy, and third was space exploration."

Ideally, what is important to you should reflect your desire to make the world a better place in some way. Do you want to feed people? Create transportation for them? Help them look fashionable? Educate them?

If every job in the world paid exactly the same wage, from CEO to sidewalk musician, and you had to do one job, what would it be? If the amount of money you earned were the same as everyone else, how would you spend your life?

2. Where do I want to go? It's good to be able to envision where you want to be in the future, and to set goals for yourself as a way to get there.

Goals come in all sizes and time durations. An immediate goal may be to get the sales report to your boss by the end of the day. Another goal might be to stop smoking cigarettes.

A longer term goal might be to save money for that boat you've wanted. Or get promoted to division head. Or start your own business.

Goals are best when they describe an accomplishment that benefits not just you but society as a whole. It's understandable if you walk past a big skyscraper and say to yourself, "Someday I want to be the CEO of that bank and have a big corner office with a view of Central Park." While you may literally want these things, what you're *really* saying is, "I want the responsibility for directing a multi-billion-dollar bank that helps people keep their money safe and gives them loans for cars and houses, which are important to them and to society." If you can handle that responsibility, the paycheck will come on its own.

3. How do I define excellence? You should be able to visualize and describe the outcomes you want to generate. How are you going to measure success? A doctor might measure success by the number of people he or she has cured or effectively treated for their injuries. A pro football coach measures success by how many games his team has won, and if they've won the Super Bowl. An aid worker in a developing nation might measure success by the number of solar-powered electric lights installed in a village.

All of these outcomes require *standards of performance* that need to be met. To achieve the standard of performance you expect from yourself, you must keep your skills up to date, or pursue a higher educational program than the one you have now. For example, to become a bank president normally requires training in economics, business, and accounting.

The key is to adopt the mindset of excellence in your field, and never stray from it.

4. What kind of person am I? Do you enjoy risk, or are you looking for stability? Are you an innovator, or do you see yourself as preserving history? Do you enjoy managing other people, or are you happier as a solo entrepreneur?

The latter question is critical for people like Cynthia, who rise to the top of a big organization. Most organizational leaders spend the majority of their time managing other people. That's their primary job. This can be a difficult transition for hands-on entrepreneurs who enjoy getting their hands dirty, but it's just a fact of life.

There are a few people who seem to possess superhuman focus and concentration. Elon Musk runs two major companies, finds time to personally work with his engineers, engages the public via social media, takes care of his five boys, sleeps enough, and continues to stay focused on his objectives. By all accounts and from people who know him, he's a very happy man.

The point is that you need to do what's right for you.

5. What legacy do I want to leave behind? It may be depressing to contemplate your own demise, but imagine if you were to drop dead *right now*. How would you be remembered by those who knew you? How had you touched the lives of your family and friends, and people in your community? It's not necessary to be a celebrity or a public figure to touch many lives. Everyone contributes to the betterment of humanity in their own way.

After he left the presidency of the United States in 1981, Jimmy Carter, who was then fifty-seven years old—close to the retirement age for civil servants—began an active new life that includes volunteer work for Habitat for Humanity, a non-profit organization that builds houses for those in need. (Does Habitat for Humanity have a mission statement? Of course it does! It's this: "Habitat's vision is of a world where everyone has a decent place to live.") Every year Jimmy and the former First Lady, Rosalynn, go to Habitat construction sites to hammer nails and saw wood with the other volunteers. To the proud new owner of a Habitat home, the former president of the United States would be just one of the many friendly people who helped build their house!

CHAPTER 10

A NEW DAY

As the clock struck nine, the Rolls-Royce glided under the portico of Cynthia's hotel.

"Before my coach turns into a pumpkin, I need to say goodnight," smiled Alex as Winston came around to open the rear door.

"I cannot believe it's over," said Cynthia as she alighted on the sidewalk. "This has been an incredible experience! I never in my life thought I'd have the opportunity to receive advice from six legendary business leaders! Each one had his or her own story and perspective. Each one found their own way to success."

"And I'm sure you will follow your own path to success as well," said Alex.

"How can I thank you?" asked Cynthia.

"Just help people lead better lives," replied Alex. He thought for a moment before glancing at Winston, who gave him a smile and a nod in return. "Yes, I think so," said Alex, as if in agreement. He turned to his guest. "Cynthia, perhaps when the day comes that I retire, you would be willing to assume ownership of the limousine service. Will you consider it?"

"It would be a big responsibility," she replied. "Do you think I could manage?"

"I'm sure you could," replied Alex. "At the right time, I'll contact you. But until then, stay well!"

After assuming his place behind the wheel, Winston closed the door. The car pulled away from the curb. Cynthia, remembering how earlier in the evening the car had suddenly appeared as if out of nowhere, vowed to keep it in her sight as long as possible.

Suddenly a tiny piece of dust struck her eye. It wasn't painful, but it caused her to blink and look down. It took less than a second for her eye to clear, and when she looked up the street was empty save for a solitary taxicab coming slowly down the block.

The next morning Cynthia awoke with the first rosy rays of dawn peeking through the curtains of her hotel window.

The memories of the previous night were crystal clear in her mind. She felt energized and ready to face the new day and her new career. Sitting up in bed, she checked her phone. Her first meeting was at seven-thirty—a get-acquainted breakfast with a group of board members including Aretha Cooke and Ruth Paulson.

Let the games begin!

Thank You—And Please Spread the Good Word!

Thank you for reading *Leadership Transitions*! I hope it has provided you with new insights, a fresh look on how to step up into any leadership role, and important topics to discuss with your friends, family, and colleagues.

If you liked this book, you can help spread the good word and help others share the memorable story of Cynthia and her magical evening in Chicago. Readers just like you have told me they intend to:

- Post a video book review
- Buy the book for friend or colleague
- Order multiple copies for their employees or business colleagues.
- Give as a gift to a college graduate or team member on a work anniversary.
- Write a five-star review on Amazon.com, which will

boost the book in the eyes of people who find it on the website.

I'd like to hear from you!

I invite you to visit the official *Leadership Transitions* website at www.bridgeviewequity.com.

Or just Google "Leadership Transitions" and you'll be sure to find it!

On the official *Leadership Transitions* website, you'll see the latest news and comments, and have the opportunity to contact me directly. I look forward to hearing from you!

Ronnell

www.ingramcontent.com/pod-product-compliance
Lightning Source LLC
Chambersburg PA
CBHW071210220526
45468CB00002B/566